Emily, here it is! My first book has been published! Your prophecy has indeed been fulfilled! Thank you for your powerful and loving message that inspired me to try one more time. This book is the result of your obedience to God.

On August 14, 2016, I sent my first manuscript to a publisher, Harold McDougal. Dr. McDougal is a godly man who has dedicated his latter years to helping authors like me share the messages that God has inspired. He deserves honor for sharing with us his amazing talents in the world of publishing. He has become my hero by publishing this, my first book.

I0005674

Contents

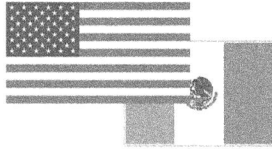

Introduction

In 1992, I met the twelve-year-old, brown-skinned boy named Oscar Mojica. I had begun teaching English as a Second Language, or ESL, to the newly arrived immigrant Hispanic students in southeastern North Carolina. Oscar had just arrived from Mexico with the very first influx of immigrant students to rural Duplin County. He had *not* been welcomed to America with open arms.

Our very first meeting occurred when Oscar rambunctiously ran into my English classroom, and, in stern, defiant Spanish, dared me to teach him English, of which he spoke very little.

Oscar was the serious, emotionally strong type of student, but something in that junior high boy's big brown eyes told me that he painfully longed for his homeland. He felt that he did not belong in America. He had *not* been welcomed to America with opened arms. In fact, many Americans considered Oscar to be a stranger who was trespassing in their country.

Naturally, Oscar longed for the familiarity of his native country and rightly so. He loved his first language—Spanish—and rightly so. With an obstinate attitude, he extended to me his dare, and I understood.

I immediately recognized that the defiant attitude this boy was displaying was only an emotional protection device or mechanism. It was more like he was daring me to try and force him to fit in or assimilate into a country which resented him just for being here. Naturally, he was deeply hurt by the rejection he felt from many Americans who did not even know him but resented him anyway.

That year, 1992, saw the first big influx or significant increase in the arrival of Hispanic im-migrant students to the rural area in which I had

Introduction

been teaching regular high school English, and, as a result, I was hired by the late Austin Carter, a beloved area supervisor, as the very first ESL teacher in Duplin County, North Carolina.

Although I was a bit nervous, I was excited about this new position. When I walked into the classroom on that first day, I was so ready to meet my new, beautiful, brown-skinned students.

When the bell rang, a group of new students boisterously tumbled into the room. While a few of them were quiet, shy and reserved, most of the rest were speaking Spanish to each other as they rushed through the door, cheerfully communicating and introducing themselves with other newly-arrived immigrant students. They were not all Mexicans, but were from a variety of Spanish-speaking countries.

Oscar Mojica was definitely braver and more prideful than most of my new ESL students, and he definitely captured my attention when he immediately challenged me upon this very first meeting. He looked me directly in the eye, and in a quiet, but defiant tone of voice, which left no doubt about the fact that he was quite serious, said, *"Le reto a que me enseñe el inglés!"* Yes, without any inhibition and upon our very first introduction to one another, he "dared" me to teach him English.

Apparently Oscar was twelve, thinking he was going on twenty. He was clearly *not* happy to be in America because he was old enough to realize that many Americans viewed him as an intruder. He had come here only because his mother had sent for him to join her in America.

Oscar's mother had come to America before him in the hope of finding work that would enable her to make life better for her precious son and his younger sister. It was a desperate measure to try to put food on the table for these children.

Before Oscar joined his mother here in this country, he and his younger sister had remained in Mexico and lived for a while with his beloved *abuela* or grandmother, two young children living in utter poverty. The house they lived in had dirt floors, and there was very little food for them to eat. Often they went hungry.

Both Oscar and his little sister had to work under extremely harsh conditions, stomping straw and donkey manure into mud for bricks at the demands of a man who had married their biological aunt.

I feel compelled to make a point here of the fact that Oscar's mother had only come to America because she was trying to escape the utter poverty of her homeland. She had only one desire, an honorable one, and that was to find work and be able to provide food for the son and daughter she had been forced to leave behind in Mexico.

Once in America, Oscar's mother had found support in a man who would become her husband and a father to her children. He helped her bring Oscar to America, and he became a loving father to the boy.

Still, moving to America was not an easy thing for Oscar Mojica. He was naturally apprehensive because he was miles and miles away from the familiar surroundings of his homeland. Although he was grateful to have left behind the extremely harsh working conditions he had suffered in Mexico, he greatly missed his homeland, and he longed for it, primarily because he so missed his *abuela*. He was saddened by the fact that he could not see his Mexican loved ones daily as before. He was *not* thrilled to be in America, but he also did *not* have a choice. His mother had insisted that he come, wanting a better life for her son. She, too, was sacrificing.

Oscar's mother missed her mother just as much as the children did. She, too, knew the pain of leaving behind the familiarity of her homeland to live in a strange country, and she would not have done it under normal circumstances.

I was thrilled to have Oscar as a student, but up until I met him, I had not personally known students who had experienced such profound hurt as a result of not being warmly welcomed by Americans. Not many Americans had said *"Bienvenidos!"* or "Welcome!" to my beautiful foreign students when they first arrived. And

Introduction

so, Oscar Mojica stomped into my room with his mind made up; he would not assimilate. He dared me to even try and make him become American. This is his story.

Loreen Sumner

Beulaville, North Carolina

And ye shall know the truth, and the truth shall make you free.

John 8:32

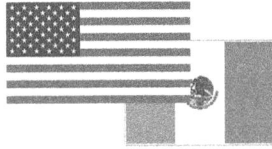

Chapter 1

Challenge Accepted

As a new teacher, I was optimistic by nature. I felt that I could conquer any negative attitude that my students presented. I could do anything I set my mind to do. As an opened-minded person, I did *not* have prejudiced attitudes toward anyone. I grew up in a loving, supportive American Caucasian family that was not prejudiced in any way.

Although my mother was born in the South in 1940, on a tobacco farm in the heart of Back Swamp, Richlands, North Carolina, she was *not* racist or prejudiced. In fact, both my mother and father were true Christians who loved their fellowman of all races and nationalities, and they had *never* taught me to be racist or biased toward any person of any origin. My parents loved and appreciated diversity, and I learned from their example to truly love and respect all races and national-ities of people from all over the world.

Honestly, I was not expecting it when Oscar Mojica ran into my classroom with such a hurtful, resentful attitude toward America and Americans. When he dared me to teach him English, in essence he was really daring me to try and make him fit in where he did not feel welcome. He didn't want to be here anymore than Americans didn't want him here.

Oscar was stubborn, but he had met his match when he met me, his first ESL teacher. What he did not expect was that I, as a new teacher, was just as stubborn as he was, and I eagerly accepted his challenge. I determined that I would definitely teach him English, and I would teach him well.

In the process of teaching Oscar English, I never intended to try to take away his Mexican heritage. Naturally, I supported his love for his familiar culture, and I embraced that culture, even as I introduced him to my American culture.

Just as tenacious as Oscar was, I wholeheartedly accepted his dare, and I immediately began to teach him to speak English. I knew that he had to learn English to survive in that American junior high school and, later, in the world at large. Coming to America as a twelve-year-old student meant that Oscar would have to learn English just as quickly as possible if he hoped to successfully climb grade levels with his peers. He would have to study more than the American students studied to achieve it. They had grown up speaking English. He spoke very little.

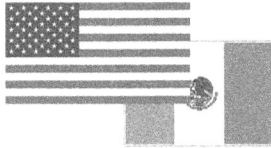

Chapter 2

The Big, Fat, Red *F* Translated to Failure

There can be no doubt that it was daunting for Oscar having to enroll in an American school. Back in Mexico, he had been studious and had made straight A's on all his schoolwork. Now he had to start over, learning everything in a strange language.

This was complicated by the fact that Oscar now had several academic teachers, a physical education teacher and various resource teachers for music and art. I had him for only ninety minutes a day in my ESL class, and I tried to understand his situation. In some of his regular mainstream academic classes, however, he began making some big, fat, red F's on some of his tests, which were given only in English.

It took time for Oscar to learn enough academic English to excel in the classroom. He was forced to quickly acquire some basic communication skills in English, but that's as far as it went.

Fairly quickly, Oscar learned to communicate in English socially and conversationally, and some of his teachers mistook this as meaning that he understood everything. This resulted in those big, fat, red F's.

I did not have to translate any of the big, fat, red F's for Oscar. He knew what they meant; he had failed another test. This was very discouraging. He knew that he was smart, above average, in fact, but how could he compete when he didn't understand enough English? He was sure he could have passed all of those tests if he had clearly understood the instructions and how to properly word his answers. He was not accustomed to failing in class. He was very studious, and he had a desire to perform well academically.

Very quickly our Duplin County School Board of Education began realizing that our changing student population meant that we needed more ESL teachers in our schools, and they responded. It was a learning process for all of us, and our county ESL Supervisor, Linda Smith, had the wisdom to quickly put into place some ESL workshops to aid in educating all of our county teachers in how to respond to this need. In these workshops, we were immersed in the teaching strategies needed to support our burgeoning immigrant student population.

Oscar was in the first wave of foreign students to arrive from Mexico to our small rural community, and teachers did not yet know how to grade ESL students, and so Oscar received those F's. Strangely, Oscar's frustration in receiving an F on an academic test worked to his advantage. He was not accustomed to failing tests. Because he was tenaciously determined not to fail, he applied himself and began to learn academic English very quickly.

Because Oscar was very intelligent and wanted to make straight A's in all of his classes, just as he had in his school in Mexico, he was determined to learn English — in spite of his obstinacy never to truly assimilate.

Oscar did not want to become an American because Americans, upon his arrival, had deeply hurt his feelings by not wanting him in "their" country. In the end, he learned English because he loved learning. His school subjects were being taught only in English, and he wanted to understand those subjects, so he applied himself and learned. He wanted to excel in English class, just as much as he wanted to excel in science, math and social studies.

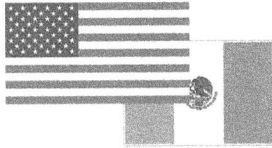

Chapter 3

Undeniable Body Language

Oscar clearly understood that many people, including some teachers, were not so thrilled that he was here in the United States. He felt that he was a burden to many of them, even to some of his teachers. Often he was all too keenly aware that he was a burden, based on the facial expressions and attitudes expressed through body language or gestures, which are much the same in every language. I did not have to translate facial expressions and body language, including rude gestures that Oscar received from some Americans, again, including some of his teachers. He knew what they meant.

Remember that Oscar was only twelve years old, but, even at that young age, it was clear to him that many people, including some of his teachers, would have preferred that he had never come to the United States. Nonetheless, he realized that learning English would help him succeed in school and in America, so he purposed in his heart to study the English language religiously.

As his ESL teacher, I was supportive of his shortcomings, but, at the same time, I knew I had to be extra tough on him. His survival depended on him mastering English quickly, and he occasionally resented the fact that I would not allow him to feel sorry for himself.

I had always believed in *The Serenity Prayer,* and I taught Oscar that he had to accept the things he was not able to change. I would not allow him to become depressed or discouraged in his studies. I held high expectations for all of my students, but especially so for Oscar. Therefore I pushed him and kept pushing him and encouraged and kept encouraging him, and taught him to persevere even in difficult times.

Oscar was often frustrated with me because I would not allow him to have a pity party, not even for a minute. When any of my students complained over too much classwork, my favorite response to them in English (and Spanish) was "*¡No hay excusas!*" or I would say, "*¡No pongas excusas!*" which translated to "No excuses!" or "Don't make excuses!"

I taught my students that it takes five years to master a language and that they would have to work extra hard to maintain the same grade level as the American students. At the same time, I did not want to overwhelm them to the point of causing them to feel like giving up, so I taught them that they would have to have patience when learning a second language.

"*¡Tenga paciencia!*" I said. I was a serious teacher in the ESL classroom, but I was also realistic. I taught the students to patiently learn one English word at a time, but I insisted that no time could be wasted. They would have to study at school and at home. So I told them they had to limit their television time (or any type of entertainment). If they watched television at home, they should watch programs in English.

Since junior high students love music, I insisted my students listen to music in English. I told them that they would have to fully immerse themselves in the English language in every possible way if they were to succeed in their studies. It was for their own good.

Every day, in class and for homework, I assigned dozens of English words for my students to learn. I called it "tough love," and Oscar sensed that I cared. He knew I had grown to love him as if he were my very own son. In this battle for his life, our hearts had become intertwined, not only as teacher and student, but as mother and son.

Chapter 4

Oscar's Eighth-Grade Graduation

In no time at all, it seemed, Oscar became proficient in the English language and excelled in his other classes. When three years had passed, he was on the threshold of graduating eighth grade. This was a very emotional experience for me. Oscar had become like a son, and the thoughts of him graduating and leaving me caused mixed emotions. I was so proud of him, but, at the same time, I was sad to see him leaving junior high and transferring to high school.

Oscar, on the other hand, was thrilled. He was graduating eighth grade and would soon be rid of Ms. Sumner, the ESL teacher who had never allowed him to make excuses or feel sorry for himself for being in a country in which many citizens by birth truly resented him. Also, he was growing into a fine young man and no longer wanted his teacher/mother to treat him as a little boy. He had his pride to consider.

On the day he graduated from junior high, Oscar proudly strutted across the stage to receive his eighth-grade diploma. With his diploma in hand, Oscar barely said goodbye as he rushed out of my life, but when he walked off stage and smiled that grateful smile, I knew that in his heart he was so grateful for all I had done to help him succeed.

Oscar and I had an understanding that went beyond language. He knew my heart, and I knew his. In my ESL classroom, he had become his teacher's son.

Oscar's Eighth-Grade Graduation

He had seen my motherly love for him in my eyes, and I had seen his deeply hidden appreciation for the genuine concern and love I expressed for him daily.

On that last day of school in June of 1995, Oscar briskly waved goodbye and quickly ran toward the school bus, which would take him home for the summer vacation.

Chapter 5

Was God Following Oscar?

The truth is that when Oscar finished junior high and was preparing to transfer to high school, I was so moved by it that I wept. I tried to keep this a secret from Oscar. For his sake, I had to pretend to be okay. Life is a struggle, I had taught him, and we have to deal with it, accepting the things we cannot change and moving on. So now I had to practice what I preached.

I also couldn't let Oscar see me crying because I didn't want him to worry because my heart was breaking at seeing him leave for high school. It was the pain a mother experiences when her child has to leave her behind, to grow into young adulthood.

That summer, before Oscar was to become a ninth-grade East Duplin High School student, I received a call from the high school principal in the small town of Beulaville. To my joy and surprise, Mr. Ken Kennedy was offering me the opportunity to transfer to East Duplin High School, as the first ESL teacher at the same school Oscar would attend as a freshman. Mr. Kennedy was aware of the influx of immigrant students who had enrolled in the junior high feeder schools, and he knew that the eighth-grade graduating ESL immigrant students would need much more support as high school freshmen. This was to be the next step in their mastery of the English language.

Was God Following Oscar?

In high school, they would need to write essays and prepare research papers, and this was a complex and demanding process for any student, much more so if English is not their first language. I joyfully accepted this offer.

I had not seen Oscar all that summer, and he did not know that I would be his ESL teacher at high school. That August, on the first day of school, he confidently and assertively walked toward room 28, which would be his high school ESL classroom. He was expecting a new ESL teacher, not his former junior high ESL teacher, who had been extremely tough on him for the past three years. When he rounded the corner, came through my class-room door, and first saw me, his facial expression immediately dropped. He was seriously disappointed.

Oscar was in disbelief now that he realized I was to be his high school

ESL teacher. He stood with his mouth agape. He said nothing at first. No *¡hola!* No hello! Nothing about his expression suggested that he was happy to see me. Finally, in perfect English, he blurted out, in his typically rude-like tone, "Are you following me?"

I smiled and said, "No, but God is!" Oscar had never liked it when I talked about God. When I told him that God had a plan for his life, he scoffed and rolled his eyes in disbelief. He may not have believed me, but I knew the truth of it. Deep inside my heart, I knew there was something special about this brown-skinned boy who was growing into a fine young man, and I knew that I had to somehow help him fulfill his purpose for being in America.

I knew that God had brought Oscar to America for a very special purpose, but he really didn't want me to talk about God. If anything at all, Oscar felt that God lacked a sense of humor

Was God Following Oscar?

by allowing his first junior high ESL teacher follow him to his high school, and he didn't really appreciate my sense of humor in pointing out that God was "following" him, not me!

Chapter 6

Becoming Legal Was a Process

Oscar was still hurt when certain Americans expressed the fact that they did not want Mexicans in "their" country. Now, as an older student, a high school freshman, he understood even more that many Americans believed he was trespassing. Even though his mother had applied for legal status for her children, Oscar knew many Americans did not want to share "their" country with him, even if he was here legally. It was natural for him not to be thrilled to be living in a country where some of the citizens felt he was trespassing, but he had not had a choice in the matter. He had arrived here as a child, escaping utter poverty. He remembered well the fact that he had barely had enough food in Mexico to keep him alive. He had come to America to survive the thing called *life*.

Now, as a young adult in high school, Oscar still did *not* feel that he belonged in America. He knew that many Americans did not want him in this country, despite his mother's determination to legalize his status.

Oscar had always been the impatient type, and he was hard on himself, pressing to succeed. Along with the other ESL students, I had taught him that it takes five years to master any language, but impatiently he had said, "I don't have that kind of time!" I told him that he would have to read a chapter in his physical science text-book five times as compared to once for the American students and taught him to carry around his English-Spanish dictionary and use it as if it were his Bible.

Back then we did not have the technology we have today, and I was forced to translate and write every word on the chalkboard. There were no Smartboards, iPads or Macbooks. We had hard-bound paper grammar books and English-Spanish dictionaries and a gigantic chalkboard that stretched horizontally across the classroom, wall-to-wall. The result was that I left school every day covered in dusty, white chalk because I had translated on that board dozens of English sentences.

I insisted that my ESL students use their pencils, or *lapices,* to copy each translated sentence into their personal English language translation notebook. It was hard work, but I was determined to help them learn English just as quickly as possible.

Oscar paid the price to learn and studied every available minute. Although he would never admit that his ESL teacher was right, he knew that I was telling him the truth, and he believed me when I instructed him that he would have to read each physical science chapter or American history chapter five times as compared to a native speaker's one. Honestly, he did it, for he was determined to excel in school.

Oscar and I were tenacious together. We worked hard, and I helped him study for all of his classes. He continued to come to my ESL class once a day for ninety minutes during his freshman and sophomore years, and he and I continued to share that bond that went beyond language. As before, our hearts were intertwined, not only as teacher and student, but as mother and son.

I was so proud of Oscar's accomplishments. Very quickly he was speaking English and reading English. The result

Becoming Legal Was a Process

was that he was excelling in his high school classes, making straight A's just as he had back home in Mexico. Oscar Mojica was on his way to becoming a North Carolina scholar in the small town of Beulaville.

Chapter 7

The First Soccer League in Beulaville

Oscar was also a gifted athlete, and he wanted to try out for the newly-formed recreational soccer team in Beulaville. Also, his new high school was in the process of adding soccer to their existing sports.

Although Oscar wanted to play soccer, he didn't want to trouble his parents to go out to the school to sign the paperwork, granting him permission to do so. It would have been hard for them since they neither one spoke English and they worked long hours to put food on the family table.

At that time, I was also serving as the athletic medical trainer after school, and I worked with all the athletes in extracurricular sports. When I came to know how much Oscar desired to play soccer but that he was disappointed and discouraged when he learned that his parents would have to come to school and sign the paperwork, granting him permission to play, for he could not see that happening, I decided to get involved and see what could be done. One evening I decided to go visit them in their home. It would be a surprise visit; even Oscar did not know I was coming.

I drove twenty miles and located the home, and when Oscar heard a vehicle entering their muddy driveway, he opened the door to see who was coming. When he recognized that it was Ms. Sumner, his ESL teacher, driving up to his house, he was so stunned that he went back inside and closed the door.

I was not offended by the fact that Oscar had closed the door in my face. I knew that he was very prideful and that he would not want me to see the conditions under which the family was living. They were certainly not as poor as they had been in Mexico, but by American standards, they were living in poverty.

Oscar was determined to have a successful life, and he did not want anyone to know he lived in a humble mobile home. He had his pride.

Also, Oscar did not want me to speak with his parents. He knew I would begin bragging on him, and he did not like that kind of attention. He was a proud young man who did not want his teacher praising him and treating him like a little boy.

Since I was just as stubborn as he was, I parked my car and uninhibitedly sashayed up to that humble mobile home and knocked on the metal door with purpose.

Oscar's mother came to answer the door. I introduced myself, in Spanish, as Oscar's ESL teacher, and began bragging on her son. I shared some of his academic accomplishments. The more I praised Oscar, the more embarrassed he became. He covered his ears, which had turned dark red with embarrassment, as my words of praise continued.

Oscar's parents were honored that I had taught their son to speak English and to excel in the classroom. They were only too happy to sign the permission forms I had taken along so that their son could play soccer. When I left Oscar's house that day, he was officially on the soccer team.

Oscar's parents found time to come to the school after they had met me. They now felt comfortable, since I had gone to their home to assure them that Oscar would be coached by some of the best coaches in Duplin County. As promised, one of Oscar's first recreational soccer coaches was a gifted coach and inspirational teacher named Betty Raynor. Betty was my best friend and an English teacher colleague. Not only was she a gifted soccer coach, but she was a concerned English teacher who desired to see unity in our small community. Thus Coach Raynor became Oscar's first soccer coach in our first soccer league in Beulaville.

This team had been created by one of our teaching colleagues, Pam Edwards, a physical education teacher in the community. The program became an immediate success, and students from all over the county came together to play soccer. Newly arriving immigrant students joined in unity with all the various local students, and they all began to learn about each other's different cultures. It was a beautiful blessing to see children of all ages and all races coming together in our small town to play soccer and become friends. God was joining the races in Beulaville through the game of soccer.

Because Oscar was a gifted soccer player with fine sportsmanship, the community began to embrace him and his new culture. He and my own teenage son Jason played on the same soccer team. It was such a joy to see different people from different cultures coming together as one to form a united community.

In keeping with the African adage, or proverb, "It takes a village to raise a child," Ms. Betty Raynor and I (along with other coaches and teachers) joined forces to mold and minister to Oscar and other young people like him. We motivated him and directed him down the right path to fulfill his godly purpose, and that purpose was to become a role model, a teacher and a coach himself for the youth of his new community, his new homeland, Beulaville, North Carolina.

Coach Betty Raynor served as a fine role model for Oscar. She was a true Christian and had the love of God in her heart. She, too, reached out to Oscar as if he were her own son. In fact, her teenage son Darryl also played on that soccer team with Oscar.

Coach Raynor and I were in the trenches, in the war to join the new immigrants in our community with the small-town home people of Beulaville. Naturally, some local town folks were unsure, unsettled and overwhelmed with uncertainty about the influx of Hispanic immigrants. The 1990s were a time of change, and part of that newness came with the foreign students and their foreign families moving into our small towns. As always, some hometown people were uncomfortable with the change.

Truly, it was quite an adjustment for some of the local people to open up their hearts and minds to the idea that immigrants from foreign countries were moving into "their" neighborhood. Change is never easy.

When Oscar began to play on Ms. Betty's first recreational soccer team, he was still new to Beulaville, and soccer was also new to Beulaville. We, as volunteer coaches and teachers, had so much to learn ourselves about the sport.

Due to losing game after game the first year that Oscar played, Betty had to give one inspirational and motivational speech after another, trying her best to keep up her team's spirits. Not surprisingly, they were having a losing season. We were a new soccer league, but we had to play a more experienced soccer league with experienced soccer players from neighboring towns and cities. That year Oscar learned how tough it is being a member of a new team in a new soccer league in a new community filled with strangers from other races and nationalities. Also, he learned how to persevere in spite of losing every game that first season. Coach Raynor would not allow any of her players to lose hope.

Finally, the losing soccer season was coming to an end, but the Championship Soccer Tournament was to be played the following weekend. Coach Raynor insisted that her players could theoretically win the whole championship tournament in spite of having experienced a losing season. Amazingly, she led her team to victory in that tournament, and Oscar received his very first shiny soccer trophy.

That night as Oscar Mojica proudly walked off the soccer field, carrying his very first shiny trophy, won from his first soccer tournament that we, as educators and coaches had newly formed, he was blessed to have had Ms. Betty Raynor as coach. God knew that she could teach him that endurance pays off and that hard work, commitment, determination and perseverance are always rewarded. That soccer trophy he earned as a result remains one of his most cherished and prized possessions to this day.

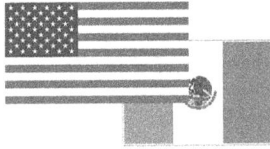

Chapter 8

Oscar's Hidden Pain Surfaced

Oscar continued to excel in and out of the classroom. He knew and Ms. Betty and I and other teachers and coaches continued to believe that he had a higher purpose in life, and we were all determined to help him achieve that greater purpose. He also continued to receive support from the educators and coaches in his new small town community. But not every American was supportive of his presence in this country, and some locals barely tolerated him, while others insisted that he was trespassing. This attitude continued to hurt Oscar, and at various times he made his hurts known to me.

In high school, Oscar had four classes a day per semester. He had his regular English class each year, and his math, science, civics, world history and American history classes were divided between the eight semesters of his four years of high school. My ESL class was a support class and one of his four daily classes. Every day for ninety minutes, I taught him how to write complex essays and research papers. We worked hard, but I understood that Oscar was discouraged and deeply hurt because some Americans still did not want him in "their" country.

Oscar was not only a good student; he was a good person. It was only natural that he resented the fact that some Americans resented him, even after all this time, and now he began to express his criticism of America almost daily in my class. This worried me.

Oscar's Hidden Pain Surfaced

I was concerned about Oscar's hurting heart as it was turning into a negative attitude. Time and time again, I reminded him that he had to get over it and accept the things he couldn't change. I told him that the truth hurts, but it sets you free—once you *know* it to be the truth. Still, he had trouble understanding why *some* people in America did not approve of him.

Oscar knew he had much to offer. He was an accomplished student and a talented athlete. And, again, Oscar was a good person. He was a fine young man who was dealing with the fact that he had left his loved ones behind in his homeland in exchange for a country with people who wanted him to return to Mexico. He longed to see his beloved *abuela,* his precious grandmother. At times, he was so very homesick for Mexico.

Every day Oscar would complain. His heart was filling up with bitterness because he was living in a country with people who made him feel that America did not belong to him. Sadly, he did not feel that he belonged anywhere. Understanding how important it was for students to feel that they belonged somewhere, I assured Oscar that I was very happy that he had become a part of my life. He was my second son, and I was his second mother.

Still, Oscar grew more and more bitter. I pointed out that this bitterness was not healthy. Again, he knew he had virtuous, honorable qualities and talents to offer America, but he was discouraged and deeply hurt because he could not prove himself to some closed-minded Americans. Every day, he would tell me to take down that American flag that hung in my ESL classroom. He had been deeply hurt by some racist Americans, he knew it was safe to take out these personal hurts and frustrations on his ESL teacher, and his deep-felt personal pain erupted and came out as criticism of America.

In my classroom, day after day, Oscar would grumble or mumble, "Take down that American flag!" He insisted that he disliked America because certain Americans resented him, even though he was working on obtaining his legal status.

Naturally, I grew impatient at times with this behavior because I personally had always been very supportive of Oscar. One day, when he was in one of those moods, I responded, to him sharply, "I will not take down the American flag. But," I continued in a softer, more compassionate tone, "I will put up the Mexican flag right next to it!" And I did.

I could say this because it suddenly dawned on me that I could put up flags from various other countries, and my classroom would represent the reality of our diversity. So I hung the Mexican flag alongside the American flag, along with the flags of other foreign countries, for my classroom represented an integration of various foreign students who had migrated to America from various parts of the world.

In the days that followed, the Mexican flag hung and waved right beside the American flag in beautiful harmony, along with dozens of flags from around the world. I wanted Oscar to know that I respected his love for his homeland, but I also expected him to learn to respect my homeland, which had now become his new "legal" home.

Still, Oscar would grumble and mumble and complain daily about Americans who hated him. Although I understood his heart and truly had compassion on him, I eventually grew tired of this complaining and grumbling. I had listened to these complaints for nearly five years and knew that Oscar had to somehow get healthy emotionally.

I would have to tell Oscar the hard truth, be completely honest with him. I told him that he had to accept the fact that he was here in America, even if many Americans did not want him in "their" country, I reminded him that God had a higher purpose for his being in America, and I taught him some scriptures.

I taught Oscar the truth of Luke 1:28, that he was *blessed and highly favored."* I told him that God's plan is higher than men's plans and encouraged him to focus on God's plan for his life and to totally ignore the Americans who did not want him in "their" country.

All of this seemed to bring little comfort to Oscar. He continued to grumble and mumble and complain about America, and he continued to insist that he disliked America ... until one day I knew I had to be more stern with him than I had ever been before. It was for his own good.

I shared with him the truths of John 8:32:

And ye shall know the truth, and the truth shall make you free.

I had to tell Oscar the truth, even if it hurt. It had to be done. I was about to say something that would hurt Oscar's feelings for quite some time to come.

Chapter 9

Knowing the Truth Makes You Free

I was tired of hearing Oscar complain about America and Americans because I knew that there were people in America who did love and accept him. I knew there were people in America who were very happy that he was here, and I was one of them. I had done everything in my power to make Oscar feel that he was a Mexican-American.

My principal, Mr. Ken Kennedy, had asked me to choose a student from my ESL classes to be a representative in the newly-created Renaissance program, which encouraged diversity at our high school. The Renaissance program was made up of students from all races and all nationalities, and we were uniting students for a higher purpose.

As principal, Mr. Kennedy desired to unify East Duplin High School, and so he had asked me to choose a leader from my ESL classes to represent the voice of our growing Hispanic student population. I chose Oscar, and he became a leader in the Renaissance program. He and the other students from various races joined together with a common goal of unity as one student body of over nine hundred students.

Oscar now felt important at East Duplin. He was excelling in his classes and had proven to be a gifted athlete. His coaches respected him, and, East Duplin had not only accepted him, but he had now been chosen to be a leader among all nine hundred students. Still, Oscar felt ostracized by some locals who did not want Mexicans in "their" community or in "their" country. This continued to hurt him.

As before, his hurt came out in my ESL class as daily criticism of America, and he continued to mumble under his breath, "I hate America!" I heard him, and he wanted me to hear him. He wanted me to do something about his pain.

He continued to insist that I take down the American flag, as if that would somehow make his pain go away. I got so tired of these complaints. Oscar was very much like my own son, and I respectfully treated him the way I treated my own son and daughter, who were students at the same high school Oscar attended. My son Jason played football at the same high school where Oscar played soccer, and the two of them were great friends, like brothers.

Still, Oscar kept focusing on the locals who did not want him in "their" country. One day, I was so frustrated ... to the point of using a very matter-of-fact tone of voice. I said to him, "Oscar, if you hate America so much, go back to Mexico!"

Oscar almost seemed to gasp. I had been so direct and truthful that I had hurt his feelings. This became a turning point for Oscar. Knowing the truth does set you free.

Oscar was greatly offended that day, but then he began to consider inwardly the fact that it was time for him to truly accept the things he could not change. As I noted earlier in the book, I taught *The Serenity Prayer* in my class:

God grant me the serenity to accept the things I cannot change;

courage to change the things I can; and wisdom to know the difference.

Knowing the Truth Makes You Free

Living one day at a time;

Enjoying one moment at a time;

Accepting hardships as the pathway to peace;

Taking, as He did, this sinful world as it is, not as I would have it;

Trusting that He will make all things right if I surrender to His Will;

That I may be reasonably happy in this life and supremely happy with Him

Forever in the next.

Amen. [1]

As was stated in this prayer, I wanted Oscar to be "reasonably happy" in his present circumstances. I was convinced that God had brought him to America for a purpose. If anyone was to blame <u>for Oscar</u>'s unhappiness and hurt in

1. http://www.allaboutprayer.org/serenity-prayer.htm

these present circumstances, it was God Himself. But, since Oscar could not be mad at God, he took out his frustrations on me. He knew that I loved him unconditionally, and he knew that my classroom was a safe place to express life's frustrations.

For months after that, Oscar pretended to be mad at me. He pouted and would not speak to me for the entire ninety minutes he was in my class, day after day. It was obvious that I had hurt his pride. In all honesty, I was only trying to set him free from his pain, but I did feel bad for hurting his feelings that way.

I now apologized every day for my insensitive comment and would sincerely ask Oscar, "When are you going to forgive me for hurting your feelings?" He never responded, saying nothing to me day in and day out.

Oscar was stubborn and obstinate and was obviously determined to punish me for hurting his feelings in telling him the truth. He would not speak to me either in English or Spanish. Instead, he gave me the silent treatment.

Unbelievably, Oscar's daily silent treatment carried on for weeks, and the weeks turned into months. He continued to come to my ESL class daily. I continued to teach and love and support all my students, even Oscar.

I attended Oscar's soccer games and track meets. (He was also a member of the track team.) I was there on the sidelines, taping his ankles before each soccer game and track meets, but he would not verbally acknowledge me or speak to me in any way. He would not even admit that he was appreciative of my taping of his ankles. He was still very offended because I had told him the truth.

Jason was playing football parallel to Oscar's soccer games, and we were winning game after game. We were still playing football the week of Thanksgiving, and that meant we were headed to the fourth round of the State Playoffs (this was in 1997). I invited some of the football and soccer team members to my house on Thanksgiving Day directly after our morning football practice. I cooked turkey and a complete Thanksgiving meal for my family and also for these student athletes. Oscar came to my house that day.

Inwardly, Oscar was touched by my efforts to continue to unite the students from East Duplin High School, and that day he finally forgave me. I think what happened was that he just forgot he was mad at me. I knew he could not stay mad forever. Now we began communicating again, while sitting next to each other at the dinner table on that Thanksgiving Day.

Chapter 10

Oscar Finally Accepted God's Sovereign Plan

Eventually, Oscar realized that I was telling him the truth, that God had brought him to America for a purpose, according to Jeremiah 29:11: *"For I know the plans I have for you declares the Lord, plans to prosper you and not harm you, plans to give you hope and a future."* Oscar began to believe the scriptures, and he accepted God's sovereignty and purpose for his life.

Back at school, I spoke to our counselor, Mr. Davis, about helping Oscar prepare to attend college, and Mr. Davis introduced Oscar to all the right people.

Mr. Davis was a God-send. With his help, Oscar received a soccer scholarship at a local university. Now Oscar was like a little bird that was ready to be pushed out of his nest, and I was the mama bird, hating to see him go.

In many ways, Oscar was very much my son. I was his second mother. Now I was an emotional wreck, knowing that he was leaving me for college. Again, I cried many tears, but, again, I kept it a secret from Oscar. I did not want him to worry about my heart. He had to go out in the real world and learn how to survive in America as a Mexican who was here for a pur-pose—a godly purpose.

As a high school teacher, I had once sung R. Kelly's popular 90s song to my students, "I Believe I Can Fly." Naturally, as teenagers, they thought it was "cheesy" for their English teacher to sing to them, but they knew better than to ridicule my singing. They could make fun of my teaching because I had given them permission, but they knew I was sensitive about my singing, so they didn't dare snicker when I sang.

I still remember the lyrics to that popular song. They are powerful, and they profoundly touched each and every student. Those lyrics became personally meaningful. They also became a believable message as Oscar was about to graduate high school and prepare to attend college. He began to believe that he could fly.

Oscar finally trusted me in my belief that God had brought him to America for a significant purpose. I constantly shared the following scriptures, which he received, and with that, he flew away to college with the Word of God buried deep in his heart:

For as the heavens are higher than the earth, so are my ways higher than your ways, and my thoughts than your thoughts.   Isaiah 55:9

There shall not any man be able to stand before thee all the days of thy life: as I was with Moses, so I will be with thee: I will not fail thee, nor forsake thee.   Joshua 1:5

Chapter 11

Leaving His Comfortable Nest

In 1999, Oscar graduated high school with honors. He was now a North Carolina Scholar and received a scholarship to play soccer at nearby Mt. Olive University, where he worked toward a criminal justice degree.

Through this period of Oscar's life, he and I remained close. He was my student/son and would visit me often. He still needed editing help with his writing, even though he was now in college. I helped him revise and revise and edit and edit.

Whenever Oscar knocked on my door, I would open it and pretend to be agitated with him. "What do you need, Oscar?" I would demand.

He would smile and say, "I have missed you, Ms. Sumner, so I just came by to visit." Then he would begin to tell me about an assignment that needed to be edited. Needless to say, Oscar was also excelling in his college classes.

Oscar graduated from Mt. Olive University of North Carolina with a four-year criminal justice degree, and, after college joined the real world, working for the sheriff of Duplin County.

Now everyone knew who Oscar was, for he was a respected citizen of the community, he was a productive citizen of the community, and he was an honorable citizen of the United States of America. Having benefited from our school system, he was now giving back to the community that had helped him when he desperately needed the support.

Interestingly enough, Oscar was also teaching English as a Second Language at a local community college, James Sprunt. He was now a grown man who had spread his wings to fly. Little did I know it at the time, but Oscar Mojica was about to leave me again. This time he would be departing from our shores.

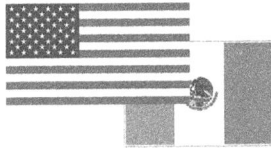

Chapter 12

Oscar Came to Say Goodbye

Oscar worked for the Duplin County sheriff for some years, and during that time I did not see much of him. Then, one afternoon, he came to see me again.

I was still teaching English at the high school, and that particular afternoon my students had gone for the day, and I was standing alone in my classroom. I opened the door and, to my surprise, there stood my precious little bird that I had pushed out of the nest so many years before. I was not expecting his visit, but it was a delight.

Oscar had come to tell me some news that he knew would make me very proud and yet, at the same time, sad. He came in with a very serious look on his face and focused on my face to see what my reaction would be to what he was about to tell me.

Oscar still spoke quietly, and his voice seemed especially gentle this day. Rather sadly and in muted voice, he said to me, "I came to say goodbye."

My heart sank. I was about to lose a son. "Where are you going?" I asked.

With obvious pride, he responded, "I am going to fight for the American flag." Unbeknownst to me, Oscar had enlisted in the United States Army.

My heart was bursting with pride in that moment, but all I could say was, "Oh, the irony!"

Then I pointed to that old American flag still hanging in my classroom and asked incredulously, "That flag? You are going to fight for the American flag that you wanted me to take down every day?"

He smiled, and I smiled, and we embraced underneath the American and Mexican flags, still hanging there side by side.

"Be careful, son," I managed with mixed emotions, as we said our goodbyes.

And, with that, Oscar Mojica left my classroom to put on the uniform of a soldier of the United States Army. I was so proud!

Chapter 13

Deployed to Iraq

Before long, Oscar was deployed to Iraq where he served two terms (twenty-seven months). During his deployment, he continued to stay in touch with me through emails.

I loved Oscar's emails. They were so descriptive, and his English was perfect. He wrote me that the drinking water in Iraq burned all the way down his throat every time he drank it. He described how the sand from the desert in Iraq literally layered his skin and uniform and became a heavy burden and the wind caused sand to cover his face constantly, filling his nose and mouth and cutting his eyes. He told me that his English-Spanish translation book (the same translation book he had kept from high school) was now filled with Iraqi desert sands. I asked Oscar what was the worst part of Iraq, and he said, the worst part was being away from his children and not knowing if he would die that day.

On a lighter note, Oscar told me he would give anything right then for a piece of that American white *Wonder Bread* (this coming from a man who had grown up eating only his mother's home-made corn tortillas).

Oscar also shared with me the serious dangers he was facing in Iraq, and I prayed for him often. A hard-working soldier, he had now become a leader in the Army and had other soldiers working under his command. He told me that those soldiers were from all different races and that he was proud to call them all his brothers. This touched my heart very deeply.

Deployed to Iraq

It also touched me when Oscar told me he often shared the lessons I had taught him with his soldiers. He repeated my favorite quotes and my favorite scriptures to them. He taught them to accept the things they could not change and told them that knowing the truth sets you free.

Oscar lost fellow soldiers in those battles and had to send some home in caskets covered with the American flag, the flag that Oscar now so proudly fought for. I worried about him, I prayed for him, and he survived the war.

After coming home from Iraq, Oscar continued to serve for another six years in the military, often stationed in Germany. I remember hearing from him one Thanksgiving Eve.

On this particular Thanksgiving Eve, I was home alone feeling sorry for myself because my husband of twenty-five years had divorced me. I was broken hearted.

Perhaps, I had allowed my teaching to consume me, and my husband and I had grown apart after twenty-five years of marriage. He was a good man and a good father, but, perhaps, I whole-heartedly believed in the scripture which states that we are to love our neighbor (or students) as much as we love ourselves (or our own children). My husband was not convinced that the scripture is a command for people today.

As a Christian, I did not believe in divorce, but it overtook us. I firmly believed the message of Jesus:

And thou shalt love the Lord thy God with all thy heart, and with all thy soul, and with all thy mind, and with all thy strength: this is the first commandment. And the second is like, namely this, Thou shalt love thy neighbour as thyself. There is none other commandment greater than these.

Mark 12:30-31

Deployed to Iraq

It was true that I had loved my students every bit as much as I loved my own children, Jason and Jessica. Whatever the case, my grown children, their spouses and my grandchildren were now eating Thanksgiving Eve dinner with my ex-husband, without their mother being a part of the holiday dinner. It saddened me that the children now had to choose between us. So, on Thanksgiving Eve in 2006, I was home alone and feeling sorry for myself.

Ironically, I was not practicing what I had preached to Oscar. Even though my ex and I had parted on amicable terms, I was still hurting from the divorce. It also hurt me that my beloved family no longer existed as it had before.

Divorce had turned our family traditions upside down, and I was left extremely downcast over it all.

Oscar was still overseas, serving in the United States Army, and it had been a while since I had heard from him.

About eight o'clock that night, the phone rang. Softly (and despondently) I answered, "Hello?" It was Oscar calling from Germany: "Happy Thanksgiving, Ms. Sumner." Oscar's voice was so warm and caring and comforting and such a needed surprise.

In that moment, I knew that I had done the right thing by supporting Oscar all through the years. He was now fighting for the American flag, and he was fighting for my freedom. He was an American in a foreign country during an American holiday, and he missed being in America. He missed his former ESL teacher, who had taught him to speak English when he was a twelve-year-old Mexican immigrant who found himself in a strange country. Now, he dearly longed for America. He loved his adopted country, and he loved me.

Chapter 14

Oscar Returned to America

Today Oscar is thirty-seven years old. He has been back home in this country now for a few years and continues to give back to the community that gave so much to him. In this way, his life has come full circle.

In fact, Oscar is back in Duplin County and is serving here as a volunteer soccer coach for East Duplin High School in Beulaville, the same school he attended. He has done this volunteer work now for years, but he continues to do it with his whole heart. He desperately wants to give back to the community that supported him, enabling him to become the fine young man he is today.

Oscar is working as a supervisor for a mental health counseling center on the border of Duplin County, and, at the same time, is working on his masters degree so that he can become a North Carolina State certified psychologist. He has used his veterans education benefits to reach his goal and will graduate with his masters in psychology in the very near future.

Oscar is also translating for and teaching English to people in several North Carolina communities, and, as noted, he has taught English as a Second Language at a local community college. In every way he can, as an honored American, he is helping other immigrants to become Americans. And, although he will always be a Mexican at heart, he is now proud to say that he is Mexican-American.

Oscar Returned to America

Oscar agrees that his ESL teacher was right. All through the years God has guided his footsteps because he is a good man:

The steps of a good man are ordered by the LORD: and he delighteth in his way.

Psalm 37:23

Oscar Mojica knows he is fulfilling God's special purpose for his life in America. When I give him scriptures today, he wholeheartedly receives them and cherishes them. He believes that God is using him for good in America.

Oscar's life is a testament to the fact that God's purpose is sovereign. From the very moment I met him in 1992, I knew he was chosen by God to fulfill a higher purpose. God had brought him to this country because He wanted to use him here. And He is using him here.

Oscar is now a proud American, a Mexican-American. He is serving God, and he is fulfilling God's purpose for his life. He now has a beautiful wife named Sonia who supports him from the soccer stands at all the soccer games. She delights in the positive comments made about her husband by the parents of the soccer players on the team he coaches and endures the negative comments. As always, some parents are extremely supportive of Oscar and his work, while others are extremely critical. Apparently some parents don't realize that Oscar is volunteering his time as a soccer coach and does not get paid to do it. They need to know that he is giving back to the community that gave to him.

For his part, Oscar is absolutely selfless in his giving. He contributes his own personal finances to many of the soccer players who need support. He just loves coaching and helping others. He is tough on his boys because he knows by experience that tough love will help these players down the road of life. He understands, by experience, that life is a struggle and that sports teaches one to endure when trials come.

Oscar and I both have learned that one cannot outgive God. As an English teacher, I love literary terms, and one of my favorite sayings is *"Oh, the irony!"* Allow me to explain:

My family and I were especially blessed in 2014, 2015 and 2016 because during those years Oscar coached my beloved nephew, Quinton Bass. 2016 was Quinton's last season of soccer under Coach Oscar Mojica, and my brother Charles Otis and his wife Emily counted themselves blessed to have Oscar as their son's coach. I was beyond blessed when I saw the skill, growth and maturity in my nephew as he battled on the soccer field until the very end in the North Carolina State soccer playoffs, giving his all on the field for his teammates and coaches.

Quinton learned many life skills from his years of playing under Coach Oscar, as Oscar taught his players to come together as a team and to work together as a team for a common goal. There could be no doubt that he taught his players well the power of unity, as the team played well into the playoff season that year.

Quinton was a leading scorer for that team, and when their season finally came to an end, he and all the other players knew that Coach Oscar was proud of the blood, sweat and tears each of them had left on the field. In the fall of 2017, Coach Oscar will return to East Duplin High School to coach a new group of high school soccer players, and Quinton will have graduated with the added benefit of having known that Coach Oscar Mojica really cared about his personal success in life.

I was beyond blessed by overhearing Oscar, as he expressed to his players from his heart many of the lessons I had previously taught him. What a thrill it was to hear him saying, "Knowing the truth sets you free!" He was able to share with his players the many struggles he had experienced in his own personal life's journey, as he followed God's plan for his life. I also overheard him calling it "tough love," and I guess he had heard that expression a time or two from his ESL teacher, along with one of her favorite Bible quotes that he also came to love: *"Whatsoever a man soweth, that shall he also reap"* (Galatians 6:7).

Truly, in terms of reaping what one sows, Oscar has been a blessing to the youth of his community, and, in return, he has been blessed with his own beautiful children that he shares with his beautiful, supportive and loving wife. As stretched as he is for time, he always puts his family first, having learned to juggle the responsibilities of life well. By day he manages a mental health counseling center, with extensions in other cities and communities, and then, after work, he gets in his van, picks up his own wife and children and several other soccer players, and the whole family goes to the Beulaville soccer games. Part of the quality time he spends with his family is spent on the soccer field, for some of his own children play.

I continue to be amazed at the many hours Oscar volunteers each week at the high school. This is his way of honoring the school that contributed to his own personal growth in his youth.

The East Duplin High School Head Coach, Joey Jones, will tell you that Oscar Mojica is his right-hand man, and Coach Jones will also confirm that Oscar is a giver, a man who gives of himself and does it on a volunteer basis. In fact, Oscar was already volunteering at East Duplin High before Coach Jones came on the scene.

Oscar Returned to America

The two of them make a great team, and coaches Joey Jones and Oscar Mojica successfully take soccer teams deep into the playoffs year after year. They have even taken their team to play in state championship games.

Coach Jones will tell you that he depends on Oscar. During soccer season, Oscar is giving back and volunteering to coach every day after a hard day's work. But Coach Mojica also voluntarily coaches and financially supports his own recreational and challenge soccer teams when he is not coaching high school soccer. He and his family love spending quality family time on the soccer fields just that much.

Today, Oscar Mojica will tell you that he believes in God. He believes that God did direct his footsteps, as a twelve-year-old, brown-skinned boy who left his homeland to find his purpose in America. He is just one example of why Americans should not resent the people God is bringing to our country. I believe God has a purpose for the many Hispanics and also for those of other nationalities. We, as Americans, need to remember that some of our ancestors were once immigrants. Some of our ancestors came to America and claimed the foreign soil as "their" very own American heritage, soil that actually belongs to God, who created it.

I am writing this true story about Oscar Mojica, first, because he is worthy of honor. He has become an example to us all, an honorable American who is teaching, counseling and financially helping the youth of our great nation. He is making America great every single day of his life. Not only did he fight for the American flag in Iraq, but after he came home he has continued to serve the community in many ways. This is a story that needs to be told. If I could, I would shout it from the highest mountain.

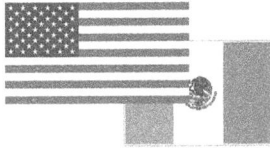

Chapter 15

I, Too, Have a Dream

If I could, I would shout, as the great Martin Luther King shouted, for I, too, have a dream. I have a dream that is the same as Dr. Martin Luther King's dream. My dream is that all nations, all races and all nationalities would come together in unity. I believe in the words of the psalmist:

Behold, how good and how pleasant it is for brethren to dwell together in unity!...for there the Lord commanded the blessing, even life for evermore.

Psalm 133

God loves unity and commands blessings on those who strive for it.

Today I am blessed because I choose to unite with all people and all nationalities. We need to truly love one another. We need to first love God, our Creator with all our heart, soul and mind, as stated in Mark 12:30:

And thou shalt love the Lord thy God with all thy heart, and with all thy soul, and with all thy mind, and with all thy strength: this is the first commandment.

Secondly, we need to love our neighbor as much as we love ourselves. That is God's commandment as well:

And the second is like, namely this, Thou shalt love thy neighbour as thyself. There is none other commandment greater than these.   Mark 12:31

We need to once again hear the heart of the great Martin Luther King, Jr. We need to shout his speech to America and remind Americans that all men and woman are created equal. It is time to come together and recognize that God created all men to be equal. He is no respecter of persons:

> *Then Peter opened his mouth, and said, Of a truth I perceive that God is no respecter of persons.* Acts 10:32

Once again, we need to hear from the heart of a man who was willing to die and did die for the freedom and equality of all men, no matter the nationality or race. Preach to us again, Dr. Martin Luther King, Jr:

Let us not wallow in the valley of despair, I say to you today, my friends. And so even though we face the difficulties of today and tomorrow, I still have a dream. It is a dream deeply rooted in the American dream. I have a dream that one day this nation will rise up and live out the true mean-ing of its creed: "We hold these truths to be self-evident, that all men are created equal."

… I have a dream that my four little children will one day live in a na-tion where they will not be judged by the color of their skin but by the content of their character.

I have a dream today!

… that little [children of all races and skin colors] will be able to join hands with [children of all rac-es and skin colors] as sisters and brothers.

I have a dream today!

I have a dream that one day every valley shall be exalted, and every hill and mountain shall be made low, the rough places will be made plain, and the crooked places will be made straight; *"and the glory of*

I, Too, Have a Dream

the Lord shall be revealed and all flesh shall see it together."

With this faith, we will be able to hew out of the mountain of despair a stone of hope. With this faith, we will be able to transform the jangling discords of our nation into a beautiful symphony of brotherhood. With this faith, we will be able to work together, to pray together, to struggle together, to go to jail together, to stand up for freedom together, knowing that we will be free one day. And this will be the day—this will be the day when all of God's children will be able to sing with new meaning:

My country 'tis of thee, sweet land of liberty, of thee I sing.

Land where my fathers died, land of the Pilgrim's pride,

From every mountainside, let

freedom ring!

And if America is to be a great nation, this must become true.

And so let freedom ring from the prodigious hilltops of New Hampshire.

Let freedom ring from the mighty mountains of New York.

Let freedom ring from the heightening Alleghenies of Pennsylvania.

Let freedom ring from the snow-capped Rockies of Colorado.

Let freedom ring from the curvaceous slopes of California.

But not only that:

Let freedom ring from Stone Mountain of Georgia.

Let freedom ring from Lookout Mountain of Tennessee.

Let freedom ring from every hill and molehill of Mississippi.

I, Too, Have a Dream

From every mountainside, let freedom ring.

And when this happens, and when we allow freedom to ring, when we let it ring from every village and every hamlet, from every state and every city, we will be able to speed up that day when all of God's children, black men and white men [and brown men and red men], Jews and Gentiles, Protestants and Catholics, will be able to join hands and sing in the words of the old Negro spiritual:

Free at last! Free at last!

Thank God Almighty, we are free at last! [2]

Thank you, Dr. Martin Luther King, Jr., for reminding us that the color of the skin is irrelevant. We should not judge people based on the color of the skin. Scientifically, all people of all nationalities and races have the same

2. http://www.americanrhetoric.com/speeches/mlkihaveadream. htm

number of melanocytes (or skin cells) which produce the *same* kind of pigment (melanin) found in each human being. Some humans produce more pigment, and some humans produce less of the very *exact* same type of pigment known as melanin, which is found in each and every race and nationality.

Skin color is based on how much protection a person needs from the sun. According to geographical location, the pigment known as melanin is produced for each human's protection. It is so sad to think that the pigment that God provided for skin protection from the sun is the very same type of pigment in each and every human—a pigment that causes such division, hate and separation.

God created pigment known as melanin to protect the human race from sun exposure. Scientifically, the amount of produced pigment varies from human to human and has sadly caused humans to divide and hate one another based on the quantity or amount of the *exact* same-type pigment (melanin) that gives each and every human being his or her shade or skin color.

Today, I am still in the classroom trying to unite the races. With my own personal, original, effective analogy, I teach my students about the pigment known as melanin by using a jar of instant coffee and a glass of clear water. With the powdery instant coffee as a representation of the powdery pigment known as melanin, the exact same pigment that each human being has in his or her body, I demonstrate how racism based on skin color differences is upheld by ignorance. I effectively tear down racism. I add a little of the coffee (brown melanin pigment) to a glass of clear water. Then I continue to add more and more coffee (brown melanin pigment) until the clear water begins to take on the color or various shades of brown, depending upon how much coffee (brown pigment known as melanin) I add to the water. This is an effective analogy which opens up the mind of closed-minded people who think that the difference in the shade or color of the skin, which is colored by the *exact* same type of brown pigment known as melanin, is a reason to divide and hate one another.

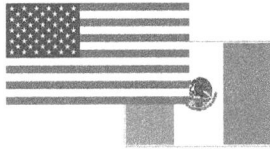

Chapter 16

Ignorance is Not Always Bliss

Ignorance is NOT always bliss. God said through the prophet Hosea:

My people are destroyed for lack of knowledge ... . Hosea 4:6

Today, more than ever, we need to educate ourselves and read the scientific studies that prove that we, as human beings, are more alike than we might think:

Human skin is normally never truly white, though some people have less melanin in their skin than others. Surprisingly, all humans, regardless of the shade ("color") of their skin, have approximately the same number of melanocytes [skin cells] per square inch of skin.

Even albinos have melanocytes, but they produce colorless, rather than pigmented, melanosomes.

Some people have darker skin than others, not because they have more melanocytes, but because they retain a greater amount of melanin ... retaining more pigment is still advantageous. People with darker skin are more resistant to sunburns and skin cancer.

... Like the miraculous plant that God provided to shade Jonah, each umbrella in our skin is a miracle for which we *"have not labored, nor made it grow"* (Jonah 4:10). We are no more deserving of this merciful, God-given shade than Jonah was.

Ignorance is Not Always Bliss

Let us then give thanks for all the undeserved provisions that God has given us through Christ, who protects and sustains both our body and soul from all that might harm us. Truly, *"He is not far from each one of us; for in Him we live and move and have our being"* (Acts 17:27–28). [3]

Also, we should not question or resent the purpose of God. God is bringing all nationalities together, and we will witness the coming of the Lord together, as stated by the prophet Isaiah:

And the glory of the LORD shall be revealed, and all flesh shall see it together: for the mouth of the LORD hath spoken it. Isaiah 40:5

To this, I say with John the Revelator:

Even so, come, Lord Jesus.

Revelation 20:22

---

3. https://answersingenesis.org/human-body/melanin/

Today, I am back in the ESL classroom, and I am teaching a new generation of brown-skinned students. Some are from Mexico, some are from Guatemala, and some are from Honduras, etc. My teacher assistant's parents are from Ecuador. The very first lesson I teach my ESL students is that one country is not better than another. We are all equal. In fact, I pull up a map on the Smartboard, and the majority of my students are connected in a circular, connecting format. Mexico touches Guatemala, Guatemala touches Honduras, etc.

I teach my students that *la tierra es la tierra,* or dirt is dirt. We all come from dirt, and we all will return to dirt, as is stated in Genesis, the book of beginnings:

In the sweat of thy face shalt thou eat bread, till thou return unto the ground; for out of it wast thou taken: for dust thou art, and unto dust shalt thou return. Genesis 3:19

Ignorance is Not Always Bliss

I take my students outside, and we examine *la tierra,* the dirt or soil, because some of my ESL students are naturally prideful when they arrive in America and think their country is superior to the other students' Latino countries. Some of my Latinos also think that their particular Spanish dialect is superior to their classmates' Spanish dialects.

When we go outside together and scoop up *la tierra,* or dirt or soil, and we all touch it, we realize how great God is and how insignificant we are in comparison to our Creator.

I love to create unity in my class among the ESL students from the various Latino countries, and that is my very first goal. Unity is so precious in the sight of God, until God commands the blessing wherever He finds it.

I love to begin my very first lesson with a visual representation of the map of Mexico, Guatemala and Honduras—the locations where most of my students were born. When I complete my lesson, all of them realize that their birth city is just a dot on the map, much as Beulaville, North Carolina, and their high school is. And yet it unites students from all over the world.

I teach my students that we are all created equal in the sight of God, that He formed the first man from dirt, and that we are all descendants of that first man, Adam. It is an absurd idea for man to think so highly of himself that he can feel superior to his fellowman who is formed from the same dirt.

May I leave you with a song that I composed some years ago. This song is dedicated to Oscar Mojica, the now grown man who first came to America from Mexico as a brown-skinned, twelve-year-old boy. He dared me to teach him English, and I did just that!

Ignorance is Not Always Bliss

Do You See It Like It Is?

When you see your fellowman—red or brown or black or white …

By the color of his skin, do you judge him wrong or right?

Do you tolerate the sight of him or do you choose to fight?

Well, have you ever looked inside of him at the color of his heart?

Do you see it like it is?

Let's tear down dividing walls that cause us separation.

All for one and one for all.

Let's stop discrimination.

Do you see it like it is?

It's time to see it like it is!

Oh, do you see it like it is?

It's time to see it like it is!

Is it a matter of the mind that's keeping us apart?

Why can't we be color blind and see things with our hearts?

Do you see it like it is?

Come on and see it like it is!

It's time to see it like it is!

Do you see it like it is?

A Special Acknowledgment

Before closing this book, I must acknowledge the importance and contribution of one more person to this story. He is Mr. Darryl Grubbs, the first principal I served under. We were especially close because there was no place for my first ESL classroom, and so I had to share a long, oblong-shaped room with him and the school's caring guidance counselor, Ms. Johnnie Boyette. As a new teacher, I felt a bit disappointed with not having my own classroom, but the county had been caught off-guard by the sudden influx of immigrant students, and we were doing the best we could.

Mr. Grubbs sat in one corner of that room, Ms. Johnnie sat in another corner, and I sat in the middle of the room, with my ESL students gathered around a horseshoe-shaped table.

After the students had left that first day, Mr. Grubbs said something to me that proved to be very important. He had been busy in his corner of the room, and I had not realized that he was paying close attention to what was transpiring with my students. Now he said, "Ms. Sumner, you need to challenge your students."

This comment came soon after Oscar Mojica had challenged me, daring me to teach him English. And so now the challenge was on, and the school principal was on my side. Oscar Mojica did not stand a chance. He would learn English in spite of the fact that he did not feel at home in America. Thank you, Mr. Grubbs, for your support.

Author Contact Page

You may contact the author at the following address:

Loreen Sumner

P.O. Box 649

Beulaville, NC 28518